I LOVE RIDING LESSONS

Coloring Book

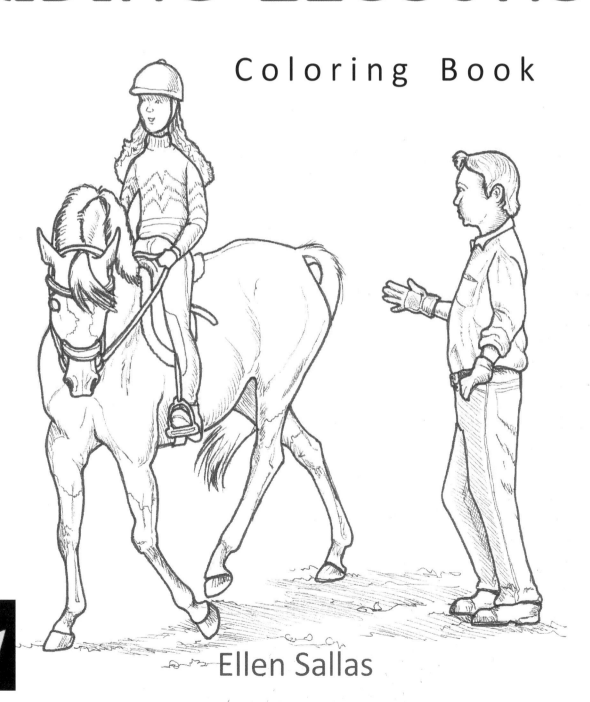

Ellen Sallas

ISBN-13: 978-0692636626
ISBN-10: 0692636625

Little Roni Publishers / Byhalia, MS
www.littleronipublishers.com
@LittleRoniPublishers

Written and illustrated by Ellen Sallas, a.k.a Ellen C. Maze

PRINTED IN THE UNITED STATES OF AMERICA

"I wear a helmet, gloves, breeches, and rubber boots for my riding lessons. When I get to the barn, I have to pet Doodle, the dog, and all of the barn cats."

~ Stanley, 8

"I always catch Flower myself. She lives in a huge pasture with the other lesson horses. I take her halter, a lead rope, and a carrot, and that's all I ever need."

~ Evelyn, 11

"My sister and I both take lessons on Halo. We tie him to the rail with a safety knot and then groom him with brushes and currycombs. He closes his eyes as if he's getting an awesome massage as we work." ~ Billy, 13, with Steph, 14

"Patches is my horse. He used to be an event horse, so I'm learning how to jump on him. I pick his hooves out before and after every ride. This is important for his foot health. I let him munch hay while I pick, because it keeps him from moving around too much." ~ Becky, 14

"I just learned how to put on Pebble's saddle. She walks very slowly when I ride her. I think we should call her Turtle. One day I will teach her to go faster."

~ Roderick, 5

"Samson is taller than I am, but he lowers his head and stands very still while I put on his bridle. I gently put my thumb in the corner of his mouth to get him to take the bit. He doesn't seem to mind. I like the way he closes his eyes as I work."

~ Sally Ann, 15

"The first thing Coach tells us to do in our lesson is to warm up at the walk. Keeping Lancelot on the rail is sometimes a chore. Coach taught me how to use my leg to make him stay on the rail and go deep into the corners." ~ Kiera, 12

"In the round pen, I drop my stirrups, cross them, and knot my reins. Then, I ask Casper to trot. Coach tells me to hold the pommel and pull myself into it. My balance is getting better and better every lesson." ~ Charlie, 9

"Jelly Bean is very careful when he steps over the ground poles. One day, I'm going to learn how to jump, too." ~ Iris, 6

"The cavaletti are my favorite part of every lesson. They have different levels; you just roll them over to change the height. Next week, I'm going to jump them, but today, we're perfecting the trot-through. Squirrely is a very nimble school horse!" ~ Sharday, 11

"Coach says that my pony needs to stop when I ask him to, so today she's teaching us to back up. It will improve Rascal's balance and build strength in his hindquarters." ~ Mary, 8

"Knotting my reins while on the longe line, Coach tells me to hold the pommel with my outside hand and press my inside hand into the small of my back. This reminds me to sit straight and tall, while keeping my leg long and heel down. Practice, practice, practice!" ~ Ryan, 16, on StarMan

"I have learned to use my legs to get Gongshow to turn. If he gets heavy on his forehand, I give tiny half-halts on the outside rein and he lifts. If he stiffens his jaw in the turn, I give a tiny squeeze-release on the inside rein and he softens. Coach said we are almost ready for our first dressage show."

~Rhonda, 13

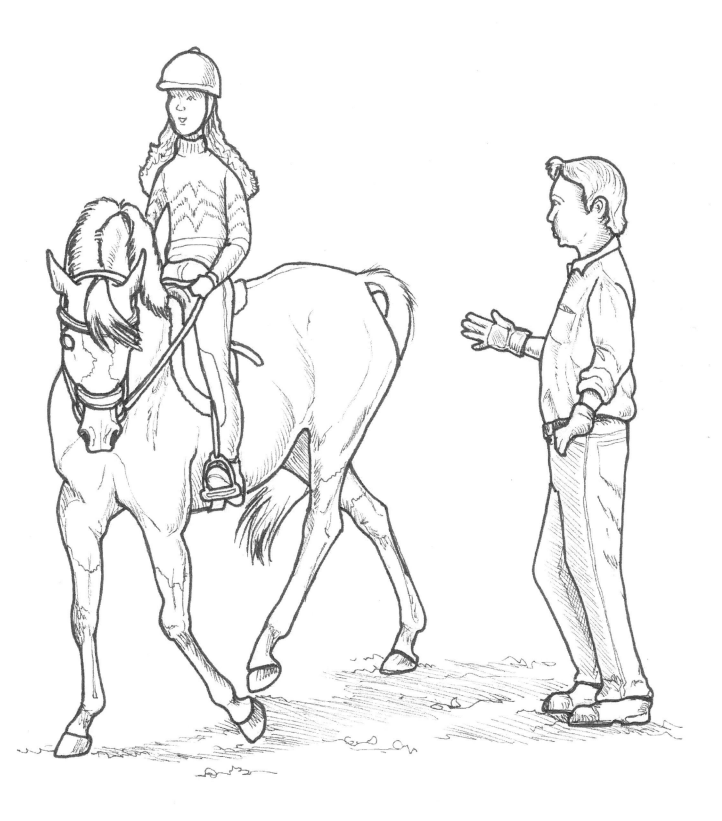

"I was only jumping on the longe, but today we're doing it on our own. Coach told me to jump the cross-rail. I cantered up, sunk down in my heel, pressed my hands into the crest of her neck, and stayed over Tess's center all the way through. I love to jump!"

~ Shannon, 13

"Petey is a retired racehorse and sometimes runs through my hand. Coach stands in the center of the ring and calls out what I should do to fix his behavior. Here, he had dunked his head down. She said lift my hands and push him into my leg. Once I did, he re-balanced. He will be an awesome jumper when we finish his training!"

~ Hildy, 14

"My entire lesson group is training for a combined training event next month. Coach told us to come out in our dressage saddles, cross our stirrups, and practice the sitting trot a while. It is hard work, and crazy bouncy on 16-hand Judah. I'm getting better every day, and Judah is never pokey." ~ Yolanda, 12

"Coach trailered me to my first horse show and gave me pointers in the warm-up ring. I was able to canter quietly around her, even with all the noise and distractions. She said it was because we had trained so well beforehand. I love my coach!"

~ Ginny, 16, on Hepsibah

"Jabba is half-Percheron, so getting him to jump takes a lot of leg. Because of that, Coach sets up combinations and single verticals during our lessons to keep him thinking and interested. He's jumping 2'6" now, so we're going to enter some events this spring." ~ Thelma, 13

"Starfish has been eventing for years, but I just started this fall. Coach told me to sit deep and sink my weight into my heels at the approach, then release when he got to his spot. He's so good that I'm not bobbling at all. I already love jumping cross-country!"

~ Tabitha, 14

"Choo-choo and I showed Novice last year and want to move up to Training. Today, our lesson group is working on the bank. If we can keep our balance and not hit our horses in the mouth or back going up and down the bank, Coach said we'll move on to the steps. I can't wait to try those!" ~ Sylvia, 17

"Sunshine refused the table at last week's Beginner Novice event. In my lesson today, Coach is showing me how to ride forward on the approach. I'm beginning to feel it when she sucks back so now I can encourage her before we reach the spot. She's a great horse and I love her so much!" ~ Cecelia, 17

"Tommy-J is half-Thoroughbred and an excellent event horse. Last week, he ran through my hand at the water. Today in my lesson, Coach is having me give him a strong half-halt at the water approach. Coach loaned me a three-ring elevator bit since he throws his head down when we get to the spot. Today, he only needed a half-halt one time. This horse is going to be a star!" ~ Billy Lee, 18

"Lil' Abner is an Appendix Quarter Horse and he loves the water! When we jump in, he lifts his legs up high in the air as he trots out, splashing us both quite a lot. I've never had a refusal at the water and I expect I never will." ~ Tracey, 17

"Crackers is a 14.2-hand appaloosa that I ride in lessons. He's small, but can jump anything. Today, *he's* teaching *me* how to do ditches. I was nervous, but he never flinched. We started with a small one, and then moved to this one at the end of the lesson. A good school horse makes all the difference!" ~ Shelly, 11

"ChinaDoll refused the wall in my lesson today, but it was my fault. I got ahead of her balance and took off my leg two strides out. After this, we circled around and jumped it perfectly. We're jumping 3'3" now and I couldn't be more proud of my little Welsh pony!" ~ Martha, 10

Look for these coloring books in the I LOVE Series,
from Little Roni Publishers

- I LOVE CROSS-COUNTRY
- I LOVE DRESSAGE
- I LOVE SHOW JUMPING
- I LOVE TRAIL RIDING
- I LOVE PONIES
- I LOVE HUNTER/JUMPER

REAL HORSE ART THAT YOU COLOR, FRAME, AND HANG!

Equestrian Parade

A SPECIAL COLORING BOOK FOR HORSE LOVERS

ABOUT THE ARTIST

Bestselling author and artist Ellen Sallas has been drawing horses even before she could walk. An avid horse lover herself, Ellen has been known to ride horses over hill and dale while daydreaming about stories yet written.

Ellen lives with her husband and vivid imagination in North Alabama.

Ellen has sold her art worldwide as an acclaimed animal portraitist for nearly thirty years. You can purchase prints and originals at https://www.etsy.com/shop/giddyupstudio or by email, ellenmaze@aol.com.

Ellen and Amber competing at J3 in Mississippi

Ellen and Amber at Foxwood Farms
Eventing Barn in Pike Road, AL

CONTACT:

https://www.facebook.com/ellen.maze

https://twitter.com/ellenmaze

www.ellencmaze.com

Little Roni Publishers Divisons include:

Illustrated Picture Books

Middle-Grade Adventure

Y/A Paranormal Romance

Gen. Adult/Paranormal

Non-Fiction

Puzzle / Coloring Books

Inspirational

www.LittleRoniPublishers.com

Made in the USA
Middletown, DE
11 December 2019